MW01488704

For Love to Live

Nolan Miller

PublishAmerica
Baltimore

First printing

At the specific preference of the author, PublishAmerica allowed this work to remain exactly as the author intended, verbatim, without editorial input.

ISBN: 1-4241-1669-4
PUBLISHED BY PUBLISHAMERICA, LLLP
www.publishamerica.com
Baltimore

Printed in the United States of America

A Grownup Lady

My little girl decided
That it was time for her to leave home
She thought that she could make it
Out there all alone
Not much more than a child herself
She was having a baby of her own
I wish I could have convinced her
That it takes time to become grown
Looking at her baby clothes
Some of which still looks brand new
Some of them appear as though
They haven't even been used
As soon as she started to growing up
That boy started to showing up
And soon her stomach started blowing up
I feared all along
That something would go wrong
So I tried my best to get her to stay
But she had to try and do things her way
There's not a whole lot more that I can say
But that I miss my child each and every day
The doctor said that there were complications
It wouldn't have been so bad
If she had taken medications
The pain is running through me
And it's gonna last for a while
You see I lost my daughter and my grandchild
And so what I'm telling you
I swear that it's the truth
She was just a baby
Trying hard to act the part,
Of a grown up lady.

Hungry for Knowledge

My grandfather was a slave who longed to be free
He passed on this passion for freedom and power to me
I know that freedom and power only come from one direction
I Held on to this belief like it was an infection
Knowledge brings both great joy and overall adulation
This can all be gained by a quality education
Black man arm yourself with knowledge
Figure out a way to get yourself into college
Like a runaway slave you must stay ahead of your pursuers
Knowledge opens doors that haters want to keep locked
They're aiming a gun at your head and it is fully cocked
The ammunition they use is fear, self hatred, doubt, and a sense of
Self loathing.
Beware of the wolves dressed up in sheep's clothing
You are not expected to achieve success
Not in life or in your business
And if you succeed without his assistance
He will even sacrifice his daughter to lower your resistance
Black man you are a target that they wish to control
They are like a hungry lion wishing to devour your soul
But hatred does not always have to win
You need to learn the rules of this battle that you are in
Wars are rarely won by brawn
But most often by the use of wits
Keep smiling and thinking, it will give your enemies fits.

In this Land

In this land of milk and honey
It seems a bit ironic but not one bit funny
That some people seem to have
More than they will ever need
Eating from tables overloaded
While others struggle to buy seed
The country's founders said that
We were all equally created
With rights guaranteed by our creator
This is what they've stated
But some people never seem to understand
That even God's laws can seem unjust
When controlled by an unrighteous man

In this land where freedom
Is treated like a bragging right
How many of us enjoy it
But have never had to fight
I don't speak of fighting
Upon some foreign shore
I speak about a battle
As close as your front door
You should not have to fight your government
To possess the things you already own
You should not have to go to war
Just to be left alone
If this land is truly mine
Then respect my sacrifice
Treat me fairly, look at me squarely
Let's make this land a paradise

The Light of Truth

The light of truth is shining down on you
Now everyone can see exactly what you do
No longer can you point and try to imply
That it wasn't you but some other guy
No longer can you claim that it's us and not y'all
Your house of cards is shaken and it's about to fall
Your game of smoke and mirrors have been discovered
Your shell game is ended the pebble is uncovered
Give it up, go away don't bother me today
You system is corrupt and I refuse to pay
Your moral stand is just a sham
You ask me if I give a care
But I don't give a damn!

Child Abuse

As a child I wasn't taught discipline
So I grew up without restraint
In school I wasn't well taught
So I said things like I'm ain't
Now I have children of my own
And they need to be taught
I tried to teach them from
This book that I bought
It is not very good
It doesn't tell me what to do
When one of my children
Hits the other with a shoe
So I finally snapped and I beat them
And man did they let out a wail
So now some people tell me
That I could go to jail
They say that it is child abuse
And I say "Oh what's the use!"
If I send my child out into the world
With no self control
What will be the cost?
If my children go out without direction
They will be quickly lost
So in this manner
I'll continue to abuse them
So that the uncaring world,
Will not misuse them.

Just Do It!

Her smile was like a light bulb
Her face was all aglow
I didn't tell her but
I was in love by hello
She was my dream come true
My darling I love you
My heart threatened to burst through my chest
She asked me for a dance
And I thought it was a test
But nevertheless
I dived from the top step
With my eyes opened wide
Today I'm gonna live
No longer will I hide
I know that love can be mine
And this time I'm gonna get it
Life can be beautiful
If I just let go and let it
No more fear no more regrets
No more covering up my bets
Nike said it
And there must be something to it
From now on, for me it's, just do it!

No Need to Ever Be Shy

At first glance I felt a flicker of love
But she was someone I felt unworthy of
Nevertheless that flicker turned to flame
I felt that at least I had to ask for her name
As I approached her she smiled
and I was frozen in place
trapped by her gaze
a stupid look on my face
As I tried to speak to her,
I could only manage Ur…
She looked at her friends
and just kind of shrugged her shoulder
That was all that I needed
to become a little bolder
I said "Hello, my name is Don,
and I believe that you
just might be the one."
"Excuse me" she said,
"But you appear to be, out of your head"
I said "I am part of the love patrol,"
"and there's an 'all points bulletin'
for a heart that's been stole"
"I have a personal interest Miss,
because you see
the heart that's been stolen belongs to me
I think you are the culprit,
it is so plain to see
All will be forgiven
if you give your heart to me
She said "okay
you can place me under arrest'
But locked up by your side

is the place I'd like best
Many years have gone by
and she still says that I, am her favorite guy,
so I won't even try, to figure out why,
there was no need for me to ever be shy.

The Times

It was the worst of times
It was the best of times
The homeless people had moved on
So nobody was out there begging for dimes
The price of gas was at an all time low
There was a lot of stuff happening
Everybody had someplace to go
My baby was in love with me
She said I was the center of her life
I was so proud of her I told everybody
Hey y'all take a look at my fine wife!
My kids were doing well in school
They each brought home straight A's
On my job they moved me from nights
And gave me permanent day's
This was truly the life,
Things were so good I thought," I must be dreaming cuz"
The alarm went off and I found out that I really wuz'

Do Some Time

I didn't see it coming so it took me by surprise
The slap didn't hurt
Still it brought tears to my eyes
I thought I was your world
Your "once in a lifetime girl"
You didn't like something I said
So you went " upside my head"
Speaking my mind is not a crime
Putt your hands on me again
I'll see you do some time

Wish That My Father

I wish that my father had been there
Because there were times when I really needed him
I wish that my father had been there
Instead of my stepfather who beat me on a whim
I wish that my father had been there
To comfort my mother when she would cry alone at night
I wish that my father had been there
Instead of my stepfather who got drunk and always wanted to fight
I wish that my father had been there
To buy and teach me how to ride my first bike
I wish that my father had been there to talk to
When I joined the boy scouts and went on my first hike
I wish that my father had been there
When I first started thinking about having girlfriends
I wish that my father had been there
To teach me that when you father a child your,
job never ends
Yes now I'm a father and I know how hard the job can be
And so to God I pray constantly
For his blessings to pour out like it was raining
I thank Him for keeping me around long enough
To receive on the job training

You Say

You say that you are my father
And I have to give you your due respect
But if you hurt my mother again
I'm gonna try to break your neck
You say that you are the man
You say this is your house
But that does not give you the right
To hit my mother in her mouth
You say that you're the boss
And we have to do everything your way
But when you disrespect my mother
I'm not trying to hear anything you say
You say that you work real hard
And that you do the best you can
But the way you disrespect my mom
Makes it impossible for me
To see you as a man!

A Brighter Day Tomorrow

She wears her smile so brightly,
No one would know that she's been crying
She bears her pain so smoothly,
No one would know that she's been hiding
her pain is a private thing
She would never share her sorrow
She clings to her grief in the hope of finding
A brighter day tomorrow
So the lady goes on to face yet another day
Maybe this time love will come to stay
Maybe this time love won't be denied
The lady is owed for the tears she's cried
Her life was once a daydream,
Filled with flowers and sun
Her life is now a nightmare
Her dreams have come undone
Her pain is a private thing
She would never share her sorrow
So she clings to her grief in the hope of finding
A brighter day tomorrow

Jealousy

I saw them laughing together and I did not understand
I thought that she had fallen in love with this other man
So I got really angry and I guess I came off wrong
But I soon began to see that something else was going on
My friends had tried to tell me that I ought to play it cool
But I got off on being crazy and acting like a fool
So now I've really done it
I turned push right into shove
This time I lost more than my temper
This time I lost my love

I begged her to forgive me and not to walk out of our door
But she shook her head and sadly said
"I can't take this anymore
For five long years you've turned my life into a living hell
Now all I can say as I walk away, is I'd like to wish you well"
I fell down on my knees even though I still believed
That this is not the proper place for a proud man to be
I begged her and I pleaded for what seemed like a very long time
It didn't do me any good because I could not change her mind
I cried out "Baby, baby! Please don't leave me alone like this!"
With a tear in her eye, she waved bye, bye
Then blew me a goodbye kiss
I know that it is my entire fault
I acted like a hawk instead of like a dove
This time I lost more than my temper
This time I lost my love.

A Man for Your Son

Do you remember the time
When you didn't have a dime
You were to scared to rob
And you couldn't find a job
You wouldn't go to school
'Cause they had too many rules
So you got it in your head
To just hang out instead
Trouble was never far away
And there soon came the day
When you and trouble fatally clashed
With a rock a young man's head was bashed
They sent you away for fifteen years
You learned how to swim through a valley of tears
And now you are reborn into a man fully grown
You now have the power to make it on your own
Mistakes are in the past
You vow to make redemption last
Your fragile soul has been re-won
Now stand up and be a man for your son!

A Sad Affair

Tyrone joined a gang and to prove that he was down with them
He chose an innocent victim to kill.
Taking deadly aim, his shot was sure and the deed was done
Tyrone's father James fathered many children by many different women
What Tyrone could not have known was that the young brother that he
killed
Was his very own.
Tyrone's brother Shawn was a lady's man to the depths of his heart.
One day spotting a sexy sixteen year old with the body of someone much
older.
Shawn became bolder, he quickly approached
Speaking sophisticated lines with sophisticated rhymes,
Nothing he said missed her, and so it was soon after he kissed her
Tyrone's Brother Shawn the player, impregnated his very own sister.
This sad story and many more like it
Are being played out in our community many more times that it should.
And the only way to reverse it
Is for fathers to not make babies they do not intend to raise.
Mothers allow your children to know their siblings
Even if the other mother(s) is someone that you can't stand
I think Sister Sledge deserves a hand.
We are all that we've got
And whether we like the song or not,
"We are family" all of us.

African Americans

From Africa to America
The trip was hard and long but we made it
A new class of people was thereby created
From the Gold Coast, the Sudan and all points in between
We met up on the plantations to experience pain and degradation
The likes of which we had never seen
As slaves and then share croppers we toiled in the heat of the day
We went from no pay to low pay, but somehow we found our way
Many escaped to the North but even there we encountered hate
When we would dare to ask for our share we were told we had to wait
Malcolm X and Martin Luther King
Spoke words of hope that were bold and daring
But hatred proved to be a more powerful thing
These two men, although they were great
Met their eventual fate, murdered by the forces of hate
The years have passed and left their mark
Nowadays when you speak of freedom you hardly get a spark
Today the great interest is in really getting paid
Nobody really cares about the progress we've made
We are in trouble as a people
And like Jerry's kids we need a marathon
Somebody please save the fading African American

As it Was in the Beginning

The Black Majority of the Black Minority
Resent the authority
Of those who come into our community
Spreading the seeds of disunity
Disrupting the flow of our positive pride
No Matter how many times we have tried
We just can not seem to ever crest that hill
Why should we need a congressional bill
To guarantee our rights without a big fight
We have already shed enough blood
To have started a flood
Your lust took a people who were once pure and black
Turned us into hybrids with whip scars on our backs
Your guilty shame said that you must always hate us
You preached to your children that they must never date us
The temptations of the flesh are too hard to resist
The more you try to stop us the more we exist
you are in a race that you will not be winning
The world is turning brown as it was in the beginning.

Black Boy on the Train

There was civil unrest in the good old US
During the summer of nineteen sixty one
Although I thought I was happy
For me trouble had just begun
I heard the conductor say
To the guys in line ahead of me
"Where you going to son?"
"Chicago!" they each replied with joy
Then he looked at my black skin
And said without a smile or a grin
"Where you goin' boy?"
Now we all had the same uniforms on
But because I was black he wasn't about to call me son
"Chicago." I weakly said, and with a growing sense of dread
I took my seat and started to sweat
Over a trip that I took and will never forget
The white folks were given blankets and pillows to enjoy
But only a cold shoulder was given to the boy
In Oklahoma City we were invited to dine
At a restaurant owned by the railroad line
The white passengers were told to sit down and eat
I was taken to the kitchen and given a seat
Now this didn't bother me as much as it might
But even the cook who was white
Shook his head and said that it just wasn't right
The trip progressed and we crossed the Mason/Dixon line
The conductor started acting like he was a friend of mine
He said "From now on all prejudice is erased"
That made me wonder if he would soon be replaced
He tried his best to convince me that it was his job to act that way
It only made me wonder, how much money does prejudice pay?
"I was only doing my job" is a familiar refrain

Of those who use their positions to cause others pain
I promise to always stand and argue with them
Because their claims of innocence will never resurrect
Not one lynched murder victim.

In the Jungle

You got pulled to the curb
Because you had the nerve
To go outside the hood
While you were up to no good
You got caught with a gun
And a bag full of dope
Now you're fresh out of chances
You're fresh out of hope
There's no use in your crying
Cause you're gonna do some time
I bet you don't know
It was your home boy that dropped a dime
See out here jealousy rules
And it traps the fools
If you don't watch your back
You're gonna get jacked
You don't know who you can trust
You don't know who is your friend
Out here we kill each other
Just to follow a trend
In the jungle everybody
Is somebody's prey

You didn't go to the big house
So now you're running your big mouth
'Youth Authority' they can't even touch me
So I'm gonna just chill for a bit
Before I make a big hit
Then I'll just stroll out the gate
Me and my crew, we're gonna regulate
Young brother you should have waited
Because you miscalculated

Since no money was paid
A contract was made
They reported your death on the late evening news
Just before the commercial for the new Nike running shoes
See in the jungle it's kill or be killed
Beat or get beaten
Where the young and the weak
Are the first to get eaten

First Peter, chapter 5, verse eight says;
'Your enemy the Devil is like a lion
Walking around looking to devour someone'
Drugs, AIDS and violence contribute to a suicidal lifestyle
Which devour our young at such a fast rate
If we don't stop it soon it will be too late
And in the jungle when the lion feeds
He goes to sleep with his belly full and tight
In the jungle, the mighty jungle
The lion sleeps tonight.

The Tribute

To all the brothers and the sisters from back in the days
You once had to play the parts of cooks and maids
We give thanks to you because you opened the doors
Today we're not washing dishes and we ain't scrubbing floors
In fact today we get to play any roles we choose
When we tell our own stories you best believe that it's true
Because when others write about us sometimes they would lie
When they cast us in their movies we would almost always die
No more of that because we are changing the way
Black folks are represented in the movies today

"Mantan" Moreland was a whole lot more than
Just a black funny man, he made money and
Poor "Stepin' Fetchit," they said he was wretched
Just an Uncle Tom, but his work was done
They tried their best to put the poor brother down
But his game was strong just like James Brown
They even had the nerve to say that he wasn't cool
But all the while he had those people fooled

Here's a tip of the hat to Sister Lena Horne
She was on the job before I was born
She has put in work for a very long time
After all these years she still looks fine
She played in "Cabin in the Sky" and "Stormy Weather"
That lady looks good no matter whatever

Here's a nod of the head to Paul Robeson
We should never forget the fine work that he's done
And to all the other people who had to pay the price
Hollywood didn't treat them very nice
They had to grin and shuffle and bug their eyes

But I think that we ought to realize, that
In order to be paid
The game had to be played
By rules Hollywood made
So yeah,
Things were tough for those of us
Who wear the darker shade

It's Just My Mind (Playing Tricks on Me)

You came into my life and you became my friend
Never did I think our good times would ever end
By the good grace of God
Like two peas in a pod
We started growing old together
Not gracefully or complacently
But we at least had each other for
Sympathetic company
Then all too soon you were gone
Now I walk the empty halls of time
And I search each room for some small sign
For the friend that once was, but is no longer mine
Sometimes I think that I can see your face
And as my pulse begins to race
I feel like I'm lost in outer space
Because as I turn around to see
It's just my mind playing tricks on me
Sometimes I think I've heard you call my name
As my heart begins to feel the pain
I wonder if I am going insane
Because as I turn around to see
It's just my mind playing tricks on me
Sometimes the wind upon my skin
Feels like the touch that I miss so much
But my instincts I can no longer trust
My hearts is now filled with misery
Because my mind plays these tricks on me
Old friend you must know this
You were always loved
You are always missed.

Congratulations

Congratulations
You have conquered the world
You've come a long way
From your humble beginnings
As a poor, country girl
People from all over the world
Acknowledge and exalt your name
On the world's stages
You practice and display your game
If you say that a thing is good
That thing becomes good as gold
And if you say buy this thing
That thing is quickly sold
But if you say that a thing is bad
For that thing there is little hope
And very soon that thing is found
To be at the end of its rope
To curry your favor captains of industry
Would gladly run a marathon
And yet a common every day clerk had the nerve
To treat you like you were any other African American

Ego Tripping 2002

I was made out of iron
I was fashioned from steel
Make no mistake
I am the real deal
When I was made
They didn't throw away the mold
They put it on display
'Cause it was made out of gold
I am just like mercury
Too swift for you to hold
My rhymes are so fresh
They will never grow old
If you think you can defeat me
Then step right upI will easily defeat you
Treat you like a little pup
I'll make you buy time on TV
So you can tell the world
How much you envy me
Now tell me who is your daddy?

Everyday People

Tiger Woods has got the goods
Talent in abundance and we are all filled with pride
So it is chilling to think that just a few years ago
On many of the courses he has tamed
He would not even have been allowed inside

Venus and Serena Williams give one the impression
That they can rule the tennis world anytime they so desire
And yet a few years ago their appearance on many tennis courts
Would have started a riot and a fire

Oprah Winfrey now rules the talk show circuit
She seems to have mastered the art of how to make everybody care
And yet a few years ago she would only be seen on TV
As a thief or somebody cheating on welfare

I find it sadly strange and disappointing that many of today's icons
Just a few years ago would have been trapped by bigotry
And turned into every day people just like you and me.

For Love to Live

Curiosity about love
Just killed another cat
This time satisfaction
Didn't bring him back
So you had better be careful
Before you lay a body down
'Cause within a few years
They could be laying yours in the ground
You see AIDS is a killer
That is running a deadly course
And it kills without compassion
It also kills without remorse
AIDS kills without a knife
AIDS kills without a gun
AIDS will even kill you
While you think you are having fun
So please take my advice
Because my people this is not a lie
It is great for love to live
But a shame for love to die

Gonna Win the Lottery

My retirement party is just around the bend
I've been buying lottery tickets
And I just know I'm gonna win
I don't need no IRAs and no 401Ks
Got myself a plan that always pays
And I know for sure that one of these days
I'm gonna quit this job and just walk away

With baited breath I check my numbers twice
My hands are numb and they are cold as ice
I hang my head because once again I didn't win
Gonna buy myself more tickets, and I will play again
Maybe this time will be the one time that I walk away with the prize
You will know that I'm a winner by just looking at my eyes
Until that happy day arrives I will not fail to pray and play
So that the very next day might somehow prove to be
The day I win the lottery.

Hurt All the Love Away

I gave you all the love I had in my heart
I held nothing back, I gave you every part
I denied myself to make sure that you were filled
I lay here now an empty shell, since all my feelings you have killed

I gave you all the love that I had inside me
I ignored the people who tried to advise me
You had no good feelings for me
In all of your dealings with me
You were just stealing from me
You broke my heart and it's not okay
Because you hurt all the love away

I rejected other girls that I could have had
I broke their hearts and treated them bad
You got your kicks from deceiving me
You played dirty tricks like misleading me
Said you would stay but wound up leaving me
You broke my heart and it's not okay
You know that hurt all the love away

Life can be cruel and I can accept that
I don't ask God for favors because I'm not like that
I invested all my love and trust
I got back only ashes and rust
You broke my heart and it's not okay
I just let you hurt all the love away

Just Plain Silly

I must be going blind, because I can't see myself
staying with you, not for even one more day.
I must be going deaf, because I can't seem to hear
Anymore of the things that you have to say.
Bringing me down seems to make you high
you've hurt me for the last time
I've got no more tears to cry.
I've got boots that were made for walking
now I'm going to put them to good use
I refuse to stick around for anymore of your abuse.
You can try to call me back but your breath will just be wasted
I want my freedom from you so bad that I can almost taste it.
See you around baby, but no I guess not really
if you think you can get me back
then you are just plain silly.

Lied To

Once again people have been lied to
Concentrated acts of violence
Have now been clearly tied to
The desire of the Sudanese government
To wipe out the black African population
From that part of the Sudanese nation
They do not want to educate them
So the plan is to harass and eradicate them
By murdering black African students and teachers alike
The Arab militia has made a very potent strike
African American men who have rejected Christianity
African American men who have embraced Islam
Please explain to me if you can
How the actions of the Arab militia differ
From actions of the White Knights of the Ku, Klux, Klan?

New Masters

In the African Sudan, a village is raided
the men are killed, the women raped and impregnated, the children
are enslaved.
The Arab slavers say it is to increase the number of worshipers for
Allah.
As if any God worth worshiping would accept worship that comes
from intimidation, deception or greed.
Meanwhile in the United States where thousands of African Ameri-
can men have denounced "Christian slave" names for names like:
Abdullah, Mohammad, et al
There is a strange and disturbing silence concerning this tragedy in
the Sudan.
Could it be they approve or do they simply dare not offend or anger
their new masters?

O.J.'s Blues

The District Attorney was fit to be tied
When he learned his star witness Mark Furhman had lied
Well I guess I used the 'N' word a couple of times or so
Exactly how many? Gee Oprah I don't really know
But I didn't really mean it, anyone who knows me will agree
Sure I stepped on a few necks, 'cause I had to get my due respect
I was only obeying the laws of the street

The Goldman and Brown families shed some mighty bitter tears
While the media tried to resurrect some ancient racial fears
The fear of a black man who acts like a beast
Made them want to lock up OJ for the rest of his life at least
But the verdict that cam back was not the one expected
The walls between the races was firmly re-erected

We're not finished with you yet OJ
In civil court is where you'll pay
We'll take your trophies, your watches and your rings
No we won't stop until we've taken everything
You laughed at our pain but you won't think that this is funny
After we get through with you
You will never be able to tempt another white girl with your money.

Oprah Winfrey Versus the Texas Cattlemen

Some Texas cattlemen took exception
To statements Oprah made about Texas beef
So these Texas cowboys decided
To cause Oprah Winfrey some grief
They ordered her to appear in court
While the Icons of Country music
Rallied to show their support
So Oprah packed up her belongings
And left the city of Chicago
She decided that the state of Texas
Was where she would do her show
Each day some Country superstar
Would show up and give Oprah their backing
As the Texas jury was finding
That the cowboys' case was lacking
The verdict of course was 'not guilty'
Yes Oprah Winfrey won her case
And she won it fair and square
It had nothing to do with race
Those Texas cowboys had to concede
With an embarrassed grin
That when you take on the Queen Oprah Winfrey
There's no way that you're gonna win.

Out of Time

Waited for the Governor to make up his mind
He didn't grant him clemency
So he ran out of time
So they went ahead and took his life because
They say he took the life of another
I wonder how they would have felt
If it had been just another brother
Because out here brothers kill brothers
Just to keep up with the trend
Ending Tookie's life will not make gang-banging end
If you wanted some closure
How about closing the door on hatred
Put food in the mouths of the hungry
Clothes on the backs of the naked
He was not responsible for the times in which we live
His life for another life was not all he had to give
Yeah, he led a violent life
And he never tried to deny it
He swore that he had changed
But you would never buy it
The media demonized him because he was once a CRIP
He saw himself as a different kind of soldier
Caught up in a circumstantial grip
I know what you're thinking
"How dare I compare Tookie to the fine young men who serve their
country well"
I heard about one the other day, he is also doing time
For abusing some prisoners who hadn't been charged or even
convicted of a crime
Look I don't ask you to condone the evil things he did
But he never used patriotism to keep his wrongdoing hid
No one should have to die for any reason at all

But unless we stop the hating
We can just watch the bodies fall
Crooked politicians, in name only Christians
Trying to tell us how to live our life
While they're busy cheating on their taxes and their wife
They executed him for the deaths of four people
Our government has taken enough lives
To cover up the church's steeple
This does not justify his sins and I pray to God he'll be forgiven
There is always a high price to pay when to desperation a man is driven
Think what you want to and say what you will
The troubles of this world will not be solved
By the signing of a bill
His death will allow some to sleep well tonight
Wake up tomorrow and go back to accumulating wealth
But look over your shoulder because
Your dissatisfied sons and daughters are a bigger threat to your health
Ending his life may satisfy your desire
But killing him is like stepping on an ember
When just outside your door, there's a raging fire.

Please Mister Bush

Please Mr. Bush, don't send my son to Iraq
'Cause if you do I don't think he's ever coming back
My son has got no business being over there
And besides those insurgents don't even fight fair
Osama Bin Laden wants to hurt our sons
Our kids are being attacked with a lot of big guns
The suicide bombers sneak up wearing a false smile
They blow up everything for a whole solid mile
My patriotism is in place but my heart is filled with doubt
Worrying about this is causing my gray hair to fall out
So please Mr. Bush send our kids home to stay
Where we only have to worry about their being shot on the freeway.

RIP

Cracker Jacks used to come in a box
Most times there was a prize included
If you think you can keep crack cocaine under locks
Then you are sadly self deluded
If you use it once then you're hooked for life
Forget about your husband, forget about your wife
Forget about your kids, forget about your home
As a matter of fact, forget everything you own
This drug is so strong
It makes you think that you're right
When you know that you're wrong
It makes you think that you're smart
Even when your mind is gone
You would even sell what you're thinking
If somebody would buy it
If somebody said that you could get high on dirt
Some of you fools would go out and try it
In a moment of sanity you ask
How in the world did I get this way?
If I don't get straight soon
There's gonna be hell to pay
But then that familiar urge comes back
And the thought just fades away
For some of us our eyes must surely close in death
Before we ever draw another drug free breath
Rest in peace my sisters
Rest in peace my brothers
Rest in peace my people.

Seasons Greetings

You smile at me and say:

"Merry Christmas and a Happy New Year!"
But what I very much fear
is that at any other time
I'd most likely hear the line:
What the hell are you doing here?
I was the same person in April that I am in December
And it should not be too hard for you to remember
Though brotherhood and caring is a thing that's divine
It is meaningless and empty if not shown all the time
If you would feed me only on Thanksgiving and Christmas day
By the time they roll around again
I would surely have wasted away
If only your cheer was honest and sincere
It would truly be a Merry Christmas and Happy New Year.

Stand and Watch (Our Love Slowly Die)

What we have is a love hate affair
I really love you but I don't think you care
Sometimes you act like I'm not even there
Of the fact that I'm hurting
You're not even aware
So I guess I might as well
Call it all off today
'Cause at the rate we're going
It's gonna die soon anyway
There's no sunshine only gray and cloudy skies
There's no laughter only tear filled eyes
And all that my heart can do is just break down and cry
As I stand and watch our love slowly die

I can see it on your face, I can see it in your eyes
I speak to you of love, you answer me with lies
Whenever we make love, I can tell that you just fake it
All the money that I make, with great joy you just take it
This affair is clearly over, we are not going to make it
So I guess I might as well say it's all over now
'Cause at the rate we're going it's gonna die soon anyhow
There's no sunshine only gray and cloudy skies
There's no laughter only tear filled eyes
And all that my heart can do is just break down and cry
As I stand and watch our love slowly die.

Stay or Go

In Iraq a situation has now been created
Some war critics have hotly debated
Should we pack up our things and go home
Or should we:
Stay until the last man has been killed
Stay until the last body bag has been filled
Or as some people say:
Stay until we secure a rock solid oil deal.

Take this Job (And Love It)

Take this job and love it
Because before you got this job
You didn't have a dime and you were hungry all the time
Whenever you would come around
Your friends would start to frown
And they always put you down
There is a song that says it too and I believe that it is true
'Nobody wants you when you're down and out'
Now you drive a nice new car and you're wearing nice new clothes
Your friends are glad to see you I hope you see the way it goes
Your home is nice and plush, and your pockets are nice and flush
So when you have to work over time
Remember when you didn't have a dime
Just place yourself above it
And say real loud "I'll take This Job and Love It!"

The Biggest Mistake

I never knew that a heart could ache so much and still sustain life
When you left I thought for sure that I would die
Then I met someone who proved to be incredible
Not only did she love me in return,
She actually loved me first
As time went by I found that I missed you less and less
Then one day I realized that I didn't miss you at all
With impeccable timing, you showed up declaring
"The biggest mistake that I ever made was in deciding to no longer
be your wife!"
Wrong again.
The biggest mistake that you ever made was in thinking that I would
ever let you back into my life.

The Black Star

The black star floats through the atmosphere,
The stratosphere and this place here
Shining, touching, embracing and inspiring
Shine on me black star, touch me as only you can
Embrace me, inspire me, caress and desire me
Please help me to be the man you would have me to be
I live for your love, I pray to be worthy of
A woman such as you, and every thing that I do
I do with pleasing you in mind
If you search the world over, through grass, stream or clover
You will never discover a treasure, no not by any measure
Greater than the love that I have in my heart for you.
Black star you must know that you are the only one
So shine on my love.

The Black Woman as a Queen

The black woman is a queen
As great as any the world has ever seen
From Nefeterri to Cleopatra
From queen Aretha to Queen Latifah
From scrubbing floors while on her knees
To opening doors with golden keys
The black woman is able to fulfill my needs
Black men you must desist
Never let me hear you call another
Black woman a bitch!
A black woman could be your mother,
Your sister, your daughter
And if you're lucky maybe even your wife
You must respect her and protect her
For it is she who gave you life.

My Blind Date

She was my blind date
And I thought somebody, must have made a mistake
I never had a date as fine as this
In the middle of talking, we spontaneously kissed
My mind was gone, I was in a zone
Surely this must be my last night on earth
Because not since the day of my birth
Have I ever had a night that was this good
There is no way I can go back to the hood
And be satisfied with the common every day
Life that used to come my way
I've been to the heights and I'm not coming down
I'm not giving up the new love that I've found
Players you better walk on by
Don't even think about it, don't even try
Cause I will haul off and sock you right dead in your eye
This was my girl to the end of the world
But the world ended like a light
That gets shut off in the middle of the night
One day there was love the next day there was hurt
One day I felt like a king the next day like dirt
I could not hold my drink
And so faster than you might think
My sweet dream turned into a nightmare
I said 'baby I still love you'
She said, 'humph I don't really care'
I had a sweet thing and I lost it
I had what I thought was treasure and I tossed it
But the God of love is kind
And a truer love one day I would find
A love that would forgive me when I made a mistake
A love that would not be blind and unforgiving
A love that was better than my blind date

The Family Cemetery

This is the place where the bones of my ancestors lie
But I will not be sad and I will tell you why
Whenever I come to visit them here
I always feel their presence near
And because I value them so much
I make a solemn promise to always stay in touch
I make a solemn vow to never forget them
My children and their children's children
We should never let them
Ever fail to remember that the place for them to always bury
Is right here at the family cemetery

The Game of Love

My friends taught me how
To play the game of love
Their attitudes
Made me feel ashamed of love
So when real love came
I thought it was a game
And that made me come off lame
So now I must take all of the blame
Today I stand here so all alone
Because the love that was here
Has found a new home.

The Joke Is on You!

Sweet kisses and warm wishes
Dominated my thoughts of you
Friends were shocked beyond belief
When they heard that we were through
How did we ever get to this place
I learn nothing new by staring
At photos of your face
Were you angry here
Or were you only thinking
Were your kisses sincere
Or was our love sinking
It hurts to one day wake up and find
That the joke has been on you all of this time
You're left standing there
And your life is a total wreck
As she goes dancing by
With her arms around the new guy's neck
Deceit can cut as deeply as a knife
It can ruin your day, it can ruin your life
You don't exactly know what to say or do
Because, ha, ha, the jokes on you!

The Legend of Stanley Gill

There is an old faded cross that sits on a hill
That reads: "Here lies Stanley Gill"
He met his match in a cotton patch
Drinking from my uncle's still
Because they call it a still
He thought it's not a big deal
From my uncle to steal
But surely he must have known
That his head would be blown
Right from off of his shoulders
Guess the liquor made him bolder
So he didn't use his head
Got caught stealing instead
Now poor Stanley Gill is dead.

The Rock Star

He once wrote the songs
that could make your body rock
when you danced to his music
you forgot about the clock
the way he sang as he played his guitar
you just knew that someday soon
He would be a star
Soon fortune and fame
Made the sound of his name
Known through out the world
So he bought a new life
For himself and his girl
They partied all night and also the next day
His lifestyle made a debt
That his body couldn't pay
Yes the drugs took their toll
They destroyed the Rock & Roll
Now he spends all his days
In a room where he plays
The same song over and over again
No I cannot go on
Because just like his song
This sad story has come to an end.

The Roots (Of Who We Have Come to Be)

Woke up this morning, already tasting the cakes and pies
You can tell what I've been thinking
With just one look into my eyes
Meeting new kin folks and laughing at new jokes
It's alright for a little while
But if you really want to make me smile
I mean if you really want to perk up my mood
Then just show me where I can find the food
Then step aside and watch me go to work
Now I don't want anybody to think
That I only come here just so I can eat
Because I really do like to meet and greet
Relatives both young and old
Especially those newly added to the fold
As we gather together once more to reunite
Let us make sure that family bonds remain real tight
Let us honor those who have gone before us into death
Let us also celebrate the ones that we have left
May we never forget who started our family tree
For after all they are the roots of who we have come to be.

The Sun Also Rises

As he sun begins its ascent
All who see it are warmed and charmed by its effect
As it takes its place up there high in the sky
Its presence is felt even when not seen by the eye
As it sits there it is admired and loved
Then all to soon the sun begins to descend
As it passes from sight it is mourned
But weeping only endures for one night
For joy, great joy comes in the morning.
I do not weep, I am not sad because I know these things
Goodnight my father, sleep well
Take your well deserved rest and I will see you in the morning
When the sun will rise again.

The Truth

Old world ties to new world lies.
Racial superiority? Not that fairy tale again?
Now I know you know that lying is a sin
Everybody got here through Adam and Eve
And it does not matter if your name is
Rufus, Ahmad, Jose or Steve
And if this comes as bad news to you
When it rains I guess it really pours
Get ready for some showers
No part of this earth is exclusively yours
But every bit of this earth is ours.

Things Together

It was not supposed to end this way
Our lives were not intended to be
Split into separate piles of things
Your books and magazines in this stack
My CD's and magazines in this pile
In retrospect I suspect that the problem with us lies
In the fact that we own too many things individually
Not enough collectively
I believe that if we owned more things together
Then maybe we would be more willing to stay together with our things
Thereby keeping our thing together.

Where's the Beef

I am feeling such pain
Because I wasn't given Novocain
You see America has pulled out all my teeth
And now it wants to hand me some beef
I am expected to go off and fight
Other brown people who don't even hate me
While right here at home my white neighbor
Won't even let his daughter date me
It's not like I even want her
She flirts with me whenever she can
I think that she wants herself a brown man
What she really wants is her daddy to be repaid
For getting caught playing with the brown maid

Who Is the Handicapped

I tried to help a sightless man today
He said "I work around here and I know where I am"
I was then approached by a man with sight who said:
"I'm lost, can you help me?" then he stuck out his hand
I tried to help a man in a wheel chair who said:
"I'm on my way to work and I'm doing just fine"
I was then approached by a man with two healthy legs
Who sat down on the ground and started begging for dimes
We are surrounded by people whose bodies do not allow them
The freedoms of the physically healthy but these people never say die
We are also surrounded by people who are handicapped by the fact
That they won't even try.

Why

Why did my leaders have to lie
Why did my brother have to die
A beautiful young man
Lost his life in a foreign land
At the hands of an enemy
That he did not understand
Back in the states
My sister met the same fate
She was shot and killed
While out on a date
It seems that hatred
Knows no boundaries or borders
No languages or colors
If you are considered one of the others
Then you are at risk
Of having your life light extinguished
There is no easy answer to easing this pain
When Eve mourned Abel
Did she also cry for Cain
Why is it necessary for this world to end
Before we can feel peace and security again

Words and Thoughts

Words and thoughts race through my mind
However, this thing I have found
The ability to put them in order
Presents a difficult task
The ability to do so
Has in the past somehow escaped my grasp
So do not be surprised
If I wear a dazed look on my face and in my eyes
I'm just trying to organize
The words and thoughts raging inside
My poor and aching head.

Your Girlfriend

Your girlfriend was knocking at my door
I told her you didn't live here anymore
She asked me to tell her exactly why you left
I told her that she could only blame herself
I said that you messed up when you took her bad advise
She said she didn't think that I was acting very nice
But then she looked around and asked if you were really gone
I said that as of today you were officially on your own
Then she asked if she could come in and fix me a meal
I said that she could, but only if she did it good
So much for your so called friend and their good wishes
The friend that advised you to leave
Is now washing my dishes.

Acknowledgements

I would like to thank my beautiful wife Yvonne for being patient with me while I neglected her and my chores as I tried to put this book together. I would also like to acknowledge my paternal grandmother the late Mrs. Josephine McAfee the source of my love for poetry and my ability to write.

I would also like to mention some of the sources of inspiration for some of the poems in this book: the poem Black Boy On The Train is a factual account of a train trip I took in 1961 from San Antonio Texas. I was inspired to write The Tribute from my anger at seeing the regrettable way African Americans were cast in some of the early movies out of Hollywood. While I was angered and saddened by this treatment I also came to realize that these actors paved the way for the Denzel Washingtons, Halle Berrys, and Jamie Foxxes etal. Quite obviously the poem Out Of Time was inspired by the plight of executed former gang member Stanley "Tookie" Williams. I was also inspired by the fabulous Oprah Winfrey, her trial down in Texas, her interview with Mark Furman and the regrettable incident at the French store where I believe she was actually snubbed.

Dedications

I would like to make a special dedication to my sister **Mrs. Levon Redwood Turnbough,** who passed away on December 23, 2005. In her honor I wrote a special poem called: *In Memory of My Sister*

I would like to dedicate this book to the following persons:
My Mother Mrs. Willie B. Miller
My Sister: Mrs. Mamie L. Lockett
My Aunts: Mrs. Loraine Dedrick, Mrs. Vititia Greggs, Mrs. Gracie Coleman
My Uncles: Mr. James Davis, Mr. Horatius Williams
My Wife: Mrs. Yvonne Miller
My Daughters: Mrs. Yvette Moody & Miss Jennifer E. Miller
My Son: Mr. Kevin S. Miller

In Memoriam

Mr. McKinley Miller—Paternal grandfather
Mrs. Josephine McAfee Dillworth—Paternal grandmother
Mr. James Crosby   Maternal grandfather
Mrs. Emaline Davis—Maternal grandmother
Mr. Herford M. Miller—Father
Mrs. Rosetta Walker—Aunt
Mr. Henry Davis Jr.—Uncle
Mr. Wilfred Miller—Uncle
Kordell Miller—Cousin
Lawrence Coleman—Uncle
(Also all the ones whose names I do not know or remember)

Printed in the United States
68996LVS00008B/24

9 781424 116690